I0815326

GOATs IN SPORTS

BASEBALL GOATs

KENNY ABDO

Fly!
An Imprint of Abdo Zoom
abdobooks.com

abdobooks.com

Published by Abdo Zoom, a division of ABDO, P.O. Box 398166, Minneapolis, Minnesota 55439.

Printed in the United States of America, North Mankato, Minnesota.
052024
092024

Photo Credits: Alamy, Getty Images, Icon Sportswire, Shutterstock
Production Contributors: Kenny Abdo, Jennie Forsberg, Grace Hansen
Design Contributors: Candice Keimig, Neil Klinepier

Library of Congress Control Number: 2023948500

Publisher's Cataloging-in-Publication Data

Names: Abdo, Kenny, author.
Title: Baseball GOATs / by Kenny Abdo
Description: Minneapolis, Minnesota : Abdo Zoom, 2025 | Series: GOATs in sports | Includes online resources and index.
Identifiers: ISBN 9781098285630 (lib. bdg.) | ISBN 9781098286330 (ebook) | ISBN 9781098286682 (Read-to-me eBook)
Subjects: LCSH: Baseball--Juvenile literature. | Baseball players--Juvenile literature. | Baseball players—Rating of--United States--Juvenile literature. | Baseball--Records--United States--Juvenile literature. | Professional athletes-Juvenile literature.
Classification: DDC 796.357--dc23

TABLE OF CONTENTS

Baseball GOATs 4

The Greats 8

Scoreboard 20

Glossary 22

Online Resources 23

Index 24

BASEBALL GOATs

For far more than a century, professional baseball has been considered America's pastime. Today, the **iconic** sport features legendary players who have rounded the bases of history!

From Babe Ruth to Mike Trout, some of the greatest players of all time have shaped the sport into the diamond it is today.

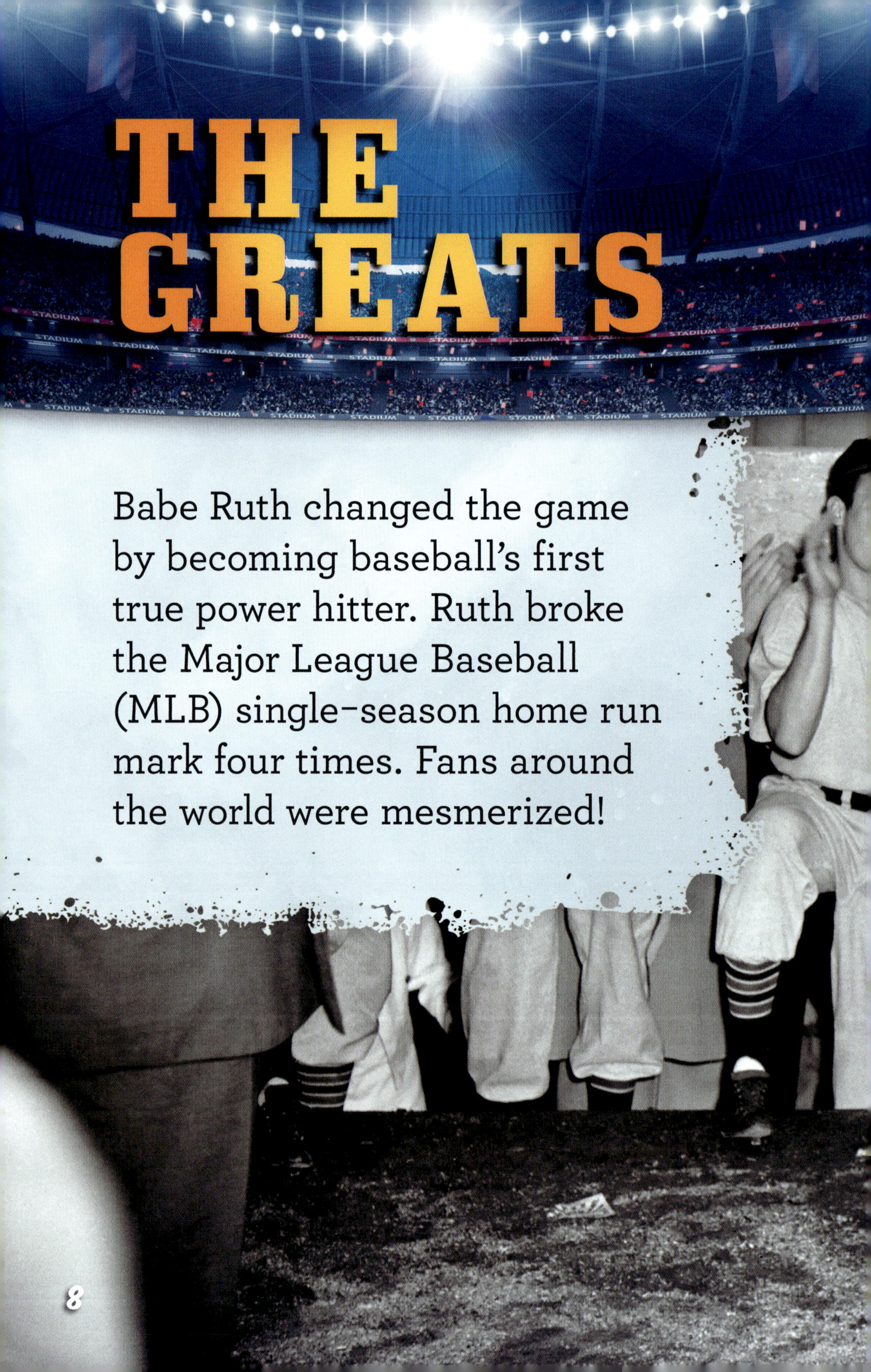

THE GREATS

Babe Ruth changed the game by becoming baseball's first true power hitter. Ruth broke the Major League Baseball (MLB) single-season home run mark four times. Fans around the world were mesmerized!

Jackie Robinson was the first Black player in MLB history. His incredible talent helped the Brooklyn Dodgers win the 1955 **World Series**! Robinson's number 42 has been retired throughout the MLB.

Willie Mays' impressive catches and powerful swing made him one of the greats. He spent 21 seasons at center field with the San Francisco Giants. Mays took home 12 **Gold Glove Awards** during his career!

Hank Aaron was a legendary slugger. He beat Babe Ruth's home run record in 1974 with 715 homers. As the new home run king, no one challenged his record for more than 30 years!

Roberto Clemente had a strong swing and heart. He got his 3,000th hit in 1972. Clemente sadly died in a plane crash on his way to help earthquake victims in Nicaragua. He was entered into the **Hall of Fame** in 1973.

Nolan Ryan ruled the pitching mound with his blazing fastball. During his amazing 27 seasons in the major leagues, Ryan collected many records, including an incredible 5,714 career strikeouts.

Cal Ripken Jr. had an incredible dedication to baseball. He claimed the record for playing in 2,632 straight games. Ripken Jr. also earned the most career home runs by a shortstop!

Barry Bonds was a powerful and lightning-fast hitter. During his time with the Giants, he broke the all-time home run record in 2007. He won the **MVP** that season and the next three seasons!

Albert Pujols gathered many achievements during his career. With the Cardinals, he won three **NL MVP Awards**. In 2020, Pujols made the top five all-time home runs list with the Los Angeles Angels.

ANGELS
27

Mike Trout has taken the baseball world by storm. He hit his 300th home run in 2020 at just 29 years old! Trout was one of the youngest players to reach that mark.

SCOREBOARD

Throughout history, athletes have wowed fans with their skills and feats. The GOATs of baseball have taken MLB records and hit them right out of the park!

GLOSSARY

Gold Glove Award – the award given annually to the MLB players who have shown superior individual fielding performances at each fielding position in both the National League (NL) and the American League (AL).

Hall of Fame – the group of highly celebrated people honored for their achievements in a sport or other activity. In baseball, it is called the National Baseball Hall of Fame.

iconic – widely known or easily recognized.

MVP – short for "most valuable player," an award given in sports to a player who has performed the best in a game or series.

NL – short for National League, it is the older of two leagues that make up the MLB. The other is the American League.

World Series – the annual championship playoff between the winning teams of the two major U.S. baseball leagues.

ONLINE RESOURCES

To learn more about the GOATs in Baseball, please visit **abdobooklinks.com** or scan this QR code. These links are routinely monitored and updated to provide the most current information available.

INDEX

Aaron, Hank 12

Angels 17

Bonds, Barry 16

Cardinals 17

Clemente, Roberto 13

Giants 11, 16

Mays, Willie 11

Pujols, Albert 17

Ripken Jr., Cal 15

Robinson, Jackie 10

Ruth, Babe 7, 8, 12

Ryan, Nolan 14

Trout, Mike 7, 19

World Series 10